T0142578

They Really Happened

Thilagaraj Kandiah Muniandy

Order this book online at www.trafford.com
or email orders@trafford.com

Most Trafford titles are also available at major online book retailers.

Printed in the United States of America.

ISBN: 978-1-4669-8200-0 (sc)
ISBN: 978-1-4669-8203-1 (hc)
ISBN: 978-1-4669-8204-8 (e)

Library of Congress Control Number: 2013903295

Trafford rev. 02/27/2013

 www.trafford.com

North America & international
toll-free: 1 888 232 4444 (USA & Canada)
fax: 812 355 4082

For my wife, Jayasree Jayaraman, daughters
T. Saritrasaraswathy and T. Ushatrra, all members of
Inba Nilayam, Parit Buntar, Perak, Malaysia, and a
friend who always scolded but was motivational

Appreciation

I would like to thank Ms. Cecilia Dharmaraj
for introducing me to Trafford Publishing

Contents

Plus Two Minus Two

On that day, just like other candidates, I was concentrating on the mathematics paper. It was sometime in November, 1970 and I was taking the Malaysian Certificate of Education Examination, a public examination taken by all students after completing Form 5 in the upper secondary level of education. I completed one of the questions, wrote +2 as the answer, thought for a little while, erased the answer, wrote -2 as the answer, and went on to complete the paper. By early December the examination was over and all candidates had an approximate three month break after which the results would be announced. I decided to go to Kuala Lumpur, the capital of Malaysia, to visit my first cousin Ragu (not his real name), who had also completed the same examination. After a few days stay at Ragu's house, both of us decided to go to Port Swettenham to visit another cousin, Mano (not his real name), who had also completed the same examination. Port Swettenham is a town located near Kuala Lumpur and its name has now been changed to Port Klang.

Mano and his family are very pious and they believe in the Hindu holy ritual called trance. Trance is defined in many ways such as 'a temporary state in which a medium, with suspension of personal consciousness, is controlled by an intelligence from without and used as a means of communication, as from the dead;' 'a half-conscious state, seemingly between sleeping and waking, in which ability to function voluntarily may be suspended;' 'a dazed or bewildered condition;' 'an unconscious, cataleptic or hypnotic condition.' The term trance may be associated with hypnosis, meditation, magic, flow, and prayer. When the Hindus use trance as a prayer, holy mantras or hymns are sang accompanied by appropriate beating of the drum and tiny cymbals. After sometime, a person who is spiritual in nature, slowly starts to dance to the singing and music and he is said to be in a trance, where as stated in the definitions, he is in a dazed and bewildered condition with the ability to function voluntarily suspended and controlled by an intelligence from without. The Hindus believe that all that is stated about trance when used for prayer happens because God or Demi-God descends into the human form, takes control and is the intelligence from without. After a person is in a trance, devotees are allowed to approach him, tell their problems and get solutions or answers, and blessings.

We arrived at Mano's house at about 10 a.m. and his family members were busy preparing for a prayer and they had invited a lady, referred to as 'Amma' or mother by Mano and his family members, to go into a trance as his family was having some problems. When our arrival was realized, everybody was happy and after the exchange of greetings and the initial fact-finding process that takes place when family members meet, Ragu and I joined in the preparation for the prayer. After lunch, Mano's mother asked us to go over to amma's house to pass some messages. We took three bicycles and rode to her house. Her house was built using wood and when I entered her house I was shocked to see that the house was built around a big banyan tree. Its roots were spiraling all over the floor and at some parts, the cement had come out. Any housing developer would have concluded that the house would collapse within a short period of time but Mano told us that Amma had stayed in the house with her family for some time and they were confident that the house would never collapse. I turned and saw amma who was sewing. I have never seen her before and at first look, I realized that there was something divine about her. She was fair skinned and in her late forties. She spoke to us in a gentle tone and she seemed to know that we were all waiting for our examination results. I thought that probably Mano or one of his family members might have told her and dismissed the thought. She continued to speak and a nasty shock awaited me. She said, referring to Ragu and Mano that their results would be good but mine may not be. I was stunned, shocked, and worried and wanted to leave the place immediately. I had studied very hard and to know that I might fail was something I could neither stomach nor digest. After telling the messages and finishing the drinks offered, we left. On the way, Ragu consoled me and Mano said that we would try and clarify matters that night when she was in a trance. Whatever consolation offered by Ragu did not work as my anxiety and agony still persisted and what was told by Mano also did not work as it was a few hours before nightfall and this thought was even more agonizing.

Night came, Amma came, some neighbours came and all of us gathered in the prayer room. The mantras and hymns were sung, the drum was beaten, and the tiny cymbals were chimed. Amma did not dance but the fact that she was in a trance was evident from her facial expressions, body movements, and speech. One by one, the neighbors and family members approached her and told their problems. They received solutions, answers, and blessings. Everybody was done and it was my turn. I walked towards her accompanied by Mano. My heart was pounding, pulse racing, throat dry and legs trembling. When we were near enough, Mano started to ask on my behalf but she stopped him. She said that she knew my problem. She asked me if I could remember that when doing the mathematics paper, I had erased one of the answers and written another answer. My memory went down memory lane and I remembered erasing +2 and writing -2. I told her that I remembered and she said that the first answer was correct and the second was wrong. She went on to say that she made me do it as she was punishing me for some mischievous acts I had taken part in but she added that I would pass but would miss by one point.

I was relieved but I did not understand what she meant by I would miss by one point. I knew it when the results were released in March, 1971. During that time, the results were categorized into Grades 1, 2, 3, and Fail. To score Grade 1, a candidate must obtain an aggregate within the range of 6 to 24; for Grade 2, the aggregate range was 24 to 34; and for Grade 3, the aggregate range was 34 to 48. If a candidate obtained an aggregate of more than 48 or if his aggregate was within the range of 6 to 48 but failed the Malay paper, he was considered to have failed the examination. I had 25 points and placed in the Grade 2 category. If I had obtained 24 points I would have got Grade 1 and this was what she meant by 'you would miss by one point' and I knew exactly why and how I had lost the one point

Some will say that going into a trance is divine in nature and its authenticity should not be suspected while some will vehemently deny it and say it is a hoax used by some to earn money. But how is it possible for a person who lived about 400 miles from me and had not seen me all through her life, tell with pin-point accuracy what I did on that day sometime in November, 1970? Some will argue from the point of 'mind reading' but when I met her I was not thinking of my examination. I am neither trying to confirm nor deny the validity or reliability of trance as I am not an authority on matters pertaining to trance but what surfaces from my experience is definitely food for thought for all.

Not This World But
The Other

Part A

My father was orphaned at an early age and was taken care of by a grand aunty who was blind. My father helped her to cook and took care of a few cows owned by her. While taking care of the cows, he used to pass by the local Tamil school and since he had an innate interest to study, he would let the cows graze and sit by the school window and follow what was taught. His action caught the attention of the estate hospital dresser and after getting to know my father's history, decided to help him. The dresser gathered documents necessary for my father to be admitted into the school and made arrangements for some financial aid. Like ducks taking to water, my father did very well in his studies. He completed his studies until Standard Six and in those days, one can get a government job after completing Standard Six if he fulfilled the age requirement. My father fulfilled this requirement since he started school late. His guardian, the dresser, enrolled him in a Tamil Teacher Training course and after completing his course successfully, was posted to teach in an estate Tamil school. After sometime he was made the headmaster of that school.

He married in 1950 and had seven children, six boys and one girl. At that time, Tamil school teachers were paid very low and to make ends meet my father gave tuition to the estate children. He charged them about twenty to fifty cents but payment rarely came. He would go house to house to collect his fees and some would pay in part while the others would say that they would pay the following month. My father would not get angry as he knew their financial status. However, he would write everything in pieces of paper hoping to collect them the following month but I do not think he was able to collect everything that was owed to him. Every evening he would spend hours reading the newspaper to improve his English proficiency and at night he would teach us to ensure all of us did very well in school. Whenever he had free time he would sit in front of the house and look at nothingness. He was worried about our future and how he was going to make it bright for all of us with the little he earned.

Since the income from his full-time and part-time jobs was not enough, he decided to improve himself academically to increase his earning power. He registered with Stamford College and followed their correspondence course and passed the Form Three Examination. He got a small pay hike but it still was not enough to take care of all our needs, which were increasing due to our increase in age. So he decided to complete Forms 4 and 5 and take the Senior Cambridge Examination as it was called then. With the Senior Cambridge

Certificate, he would be eligible to be promoted as the Inspector of Schools, which would see him earning more. Once again he registered with Stamford College and followed the same mode of study.

On the morning of February 1, 1967, my father complained of slight chest pain and irritation in his left arm to my mother. She rubbed some ointment on his chest and arm and told him to rest but being duty-bound, he went to school to teach. Half way through teaching, the pain became unbearable and he decided to go to the hospital, which was one mile away. He cycled to the hospital and the doctor told him it was gastric pain. He gave him some medicine and told him to go to work. My father cycled back to school and continued to teach. The pain became excruciating and he decided to go home. He walked the hundred metres that separated the school and our house and about ten metres from the house he collapsed and died.

Fate only allowed my father to complete part of Form 4 of his correspondence course. A few days after his funeral, I went through his Form 4 correspondence course answer scripts. He received raving reports from the examiners and I was very sure that he would have completed his Senior Cambridge Examination with distinction and promoted as the Inspector of Schools. But God had other plans for him.

A few months after his death, the government announced a salary revision and all teachers, regardless of whether they taught in Malay, Chinese, Tamil, or English schools, were put in the same salary scheme. Its implementation was backdated and as such, all Tamil school teachers received substantial amounts of money as arrears and a more than satisfying pay rise. My father, with his Form Three qualification, would have got much more in terms of arrears and pay hike and if only this scheme was announced earlier, my father would not have worried so much and possibly lived to receive what was due to him. But God had other plans for him.

Part B

After my father passed away, we went and stayed with our maternal grandparents. Three years earlier, my grand aunty, that is my mother's elder sister, had lost her husband and she and her five children were already staying with my grandparents and now with us, my grandparents had eight extra mouths to feed with the RM 236.00 my grandfather received as pension. My uncles did give money to my grandfather to help ease the financial burden but what they gave was not enough and they could not be blamed as they had their own families to take care of.

My grandparents' house was quite big and to get extra income, two of the rooms were let out to government servants who came to serve in the town that we stayed in. Besides them, there were also students who were renting in the house. These students were children of my grandparents' distant relatives and friends. They were not given separate rooms and due to this, the rental was low. They would rough it out with us. Food was provided for all and this meant extra cooking, which was taken care of by my grand aunty and mother. There were some who were not renting but wanted only food, which was provided with charge.

Income increased and so did expense for my grandparents and workload for my grand aunty and mother. Every day, from dawn to dusk, they would be cooking, washing, and serving and no matter how hard they worked, income was still not sufficient. At night, after finishing all the chores, they would get some free time and that was spent on discussing the uncertain future of their respective children and this time, it was worrying and crying. Then in 1970, my grandfather died. The family's pillar of strength and torch bearer was removed by God but my grandmother, who until then was dependent on my grandfather, decided to take the rein and torch and provide the strength and light for the family.

In 1972, my grand aunty and her children left to settle in Kuala Lumpur as her eldest daughter had secured a job in the capital town and was provided with housing facilities. There were now less mouths to feed but the cooking, washing, and serving still had to go on as the price of household items were going up, education was becoming costly, and as we were much older, extra money was needed for our personal expense. So, my mother continued to do the chores from dawn to dusk. The only difference was they were all done by my mother alone. The worrying and crying were also going on. The only difference was they were done by my mother alone. My mother was also unhappy that she was not able to give money to reduce the financial burden. In 1973, I got a temporary teaching job with a private school in my town and I was paid RM 165.00 per month. I used to give the entire pay packet to my mother but it did not help much to solve the financial strain as the sum was meager. Due to lack of funds, there were minor family squabbles and they were occurring almost daily. This meant more worrying and crying for my mother. I do not remember seeing my mother's face merry and eyes dry.

In 1974, I was chosen to undergo a two-year Teacher Training Course in a Teacher Training College in Kuala Lumpur. I stayed in my grand aunt's house and walked to college as it was not far. I received RM 150.00 as allowance and part of it I would send to my grandmother for family expenses. During college holidays, I would return home and on one such trip, my mother told me that a coconut from one of the tall coconut trees around my grandparents' house had dropped on her head. According to her, the doctor said it was nothing serious. On another trip, she told me that after my training she wanted to stay with me. I told her that I would be posted to a remote part of Malaysia since it was compulsory for all trained teachers to serve in East Malaysia for five years and that it was not developed and conditions would not be conducive for her to stay comfortably. I told her to stay with my grandmother as the environment was comfortable. I told her I would send more money. She was adamant and would not listen to me. I knew she wanted a life like my grand aunty. I ended the discussion by telling her that the best thing to do would be to first finish my training successfully.

I was in my second year of training. It was 12 August, 1975. At about 8 p.m. my grand aunt's neighbor's eldest daughter came running and told us that we had a phone call from our hometown and she went on to add that the caller had said that it was an emergency. There was no telephone in my grand aunt's house and the neighbor was kind enough to allow us to use theirs. My eldest cousin sister went running to the neighbor's house to attend to the call. One of the tenants at my grandparents' house was at the other end and he told her that my mother was hospitalized with severe headache that evening and after a few hours had lost consciousness and the doctors had lost hope. My cousin sister walked back home hurriedly and with tears streaming down her eyes, narrated everything to us. After half an hour, another call came. My eldest cousin sister ran to answer. After a few minutes, she walked back home but this time slowly. She looked at us with painful teary eyes and told that my mother had just died. In her death certificate it was written that the cause of death was a blood clot in her brain, which I think was caused by the coconut accident.

I finished my training and was posted to teach in a primary school in a small town. One night, after settling down to life in that small town, my mother came in my dream and told me that she had followed me and was staying in a small temple that she had built in front of my school. I told her not to follow me as she would be uncomfortable but she did and I was wrong. She was comfortable.

After a few months, the government announced the Widow's Pension Scheme. Under this scheme, if the husband dies, his wife will receive his pension. All those eligible in the country received their pension but my mother was not around to receive hers. If only the pension scheme was announced earlier, my mother would have worried and cried less and probably would not have gone to the spot where she had encountered the coconut accident and she would not have died. God had other plans for her.

. . . Yes I can Manage Science Stream . . .

It all started when the Lower Certificate of Education Examination results were announced. The year was 1968 and I had sat for the examination. In Malaysia, all students enrolled in government schools, after completing three years of education in the lower secondary level, are required to sit for this public examination after completing Form 3. It was compulsory for all students to pass this examination to go to Form 4. To pass this examination, a candidate must get an aggregate of between 5 to 34 and any aggregate of more than 34 means the candidate has failed. If the candidate wishes to continue his studies, he must repeat one year of study in Form 3 and sit for the examination for a second time. This public examination is still conducted for all students after completing lower secondary education but the name of the examination, criteria for passing and requirements for promotion to Form 4 have undergone changes.

My cousin, who had also taken the same examination, and I, walked nervously towards the school's office to get our results. The entrance to the office was crowded with other students who were also eagerly waiting to get their results. My cousin received his first. He was happy as he had an aggregate of 13 with a few distinctions. I received mine and my aggregate was 28 and I was much happier than my cousin because I did not expect to pass as I was not as intelligent and hardworking as my cousin.

It was Monday, the first day of the new school year and all students were at the school's assembly area. After singing the national anthem, the state, and the school songs, the school's principal gave his speech and this was followed by the senior assistant's speech and announcements by the teacher-in-charge for the week. After these, all students were asked to go to their respective classrooms except us, the new Form 4 students. The teacher-in-charge of examinations then read the names of students who had qualified for the Science Stream in Form 4. To qualify for the science stream, a student must have done well in the Lower Certificate of Education Examination. After the names for science students were read, we were told that those whose names were not mentioned would be placed in the Arts Stream. However, in that year the number who had qualified for the Science Stream was not enough to form a class. The Ministry of Education has regulations regarding the total number of students needed in a classroom to start lessons. Since the number was not enough, the principal asked if anyone of us in the Arts Stream would like to be placed in the Science Stream. A few hands went up including mine. When the number was enough, all of us were told to go to our classrooms.

Once in the classroom, everybody was busy trying to book places, tables, and chairs. This was when it happened, the turning point in my academic life. Alex, (not his real name) who was the top achiever in the Lower Certificate of Education Examination for 1968, came up to me and asked if I can manage in the Science Stream and he answered it by himself with a 'I know you cannot' cynical smile. I was insulted and felt ashamed and I decided then that I would show him I can.

So my upper secondary studies started with a one-sided battle as Alex did not know about my resolution. I was not born intelligent but I can be a hardworking student. I bought all the books needed and started my new academic journey. I paid attention to what was taught in class and revised daily. After coming home from school, I would have my lunch, rest for half an hour and at about 2.30 p.m. I would start studying by finishing all my homework and after this I would start revising until 5 p.m. Then I would have tea and join the boys for football. I would be back home by 7 p.m. and after a bath, I would start revising until 9 p.m. I would stop for half an hour for dinner and get back to revision until 11 p.m. During weekends I would add a revision session in the morning from 8 a.m. to 11 a.m. and continue with the study strategy planned for afternoons and nights. Whenever I decided to forgo revision for a day to rest, a feeling of guilt would creep into me and I would go to the study table to revise my lessons. What I was doing was consistent studying and in doing so, managed to go through the assigned text, Chemistry by Lambert, five times and I used Chemistry by Underwood for supplementary knowledge.

My grades did improve but my performance was nowhere near Alex's. I decided to be realistic. I definitely cannot be better than Alex in all subjects but maybe it was possible in one science subject. I chose chemistry. My study pattern continued with a slight change, which was more focus on chemistry. My grades continued to improve with the score in chemistry going up significantly. One year went by and we were now in Form 5. I continued with my revision religiously and grades kept improving.

Then it happened. The first term examination was over and results were released. Alex came to me to find out about my score for chemistry. I had scored 80 marks and Alex had 95. I was still behind but the satisfying thing was, Alex took notice of me and viewed me as a threat to him in Chemistry. From then on, whenever we had any test, Alex was sure to come over and find out about my score and each time he would leave with a relieved satisfying smile because I was still behind him. I decided that in the trial examination, which was usually held before any major public examination, I would give my best shot and hopefully be able to score more than him.

The trial examination was over and the chemistry teacher was giving out the marked answer scripts. One by one, my classmates went to collect their scripts. Then the teacher called Alex's name. He went, collected his script, saw his marks, came straight to my table, showed me his marks, and left not with a relieved satisfying smile but a very relieved satisfying smile. He had 99 marks out of the possible full marks of 100. I was a beaten figure and suddenly felt very tired. I gave it all I had and now I could only hope against hope for a miracle, which I knew would never happen. I prepared for defeat by telling myself that it was perfectly alright to lose to Alex as I had managed to not only narrow the difference in marks between us but also made Alex to view me as a serious contender to his reign. My name was called and I walked fast as the battle was all over and I wanted to get it over with as fast as possible and not prolong the agony. I took my paper, saw my marks, and walked back to my place. This time Alex did not come to my place and relief and satisfaction were written all over his face.

The chemistry teacher called our names again but this time to record our marks in his record book. He called the names one by one, marks were told, and they were recorded. When my name was called I stood up and told 99½. Alex immediately turned his head with a stunned, painful, and unbelievable look on his face and in reply I gave a 'yes Alex I can manage in the Science Stream' look.

From this incident two matters surface. One matter is, if you want something badly, keep trying sincerely, earnestly, and diligently and success will come. The other matter is, when you want something very badly, no one must be hurt. What took place between Alex and me was competition and jealousy but they were healthy, constructive, and positive competition and jealousy where our friendship was not strained. This is how it should be when you are trying for something.

No Matter What

Hockey was a game I did not like playing when I was in school. I played the game once and after the ball hit my legs twice, I decided to give up as it was very painful. This changed in 1975 when Malaysia hosted the world cup tournament for hockey. I was at Merdeka Stadium in Kuala Lumpur to watch Malaysia's first game, which was against New Zealand. The referee blew the whistle and the game started. The Malaysian players exchanged passes amongst them and the ball was sent to Mahendran, the Malaysian right winger. He took the ball, ran with it, dribbled past a few New Zealand players gracefully, ran some more, and hit the ball into the New Zealand goal area. He exhibited silky hockey skills and I was mesmerized with his way of playing hockey. I decided to give hockey another shot.

The following evening in college, I took a hockey stick and a ball and tried to dribble like the way Mahendran did. From behind I heard a voice asking me to join the college hockey team. It was the college hockey team captain and he said that I had the skills and wanted me to join the college team, which I did. When playing for college, the ball did hit my legs but this time it was bearable. I was enjoying the game very much and even after finishing college, I continued to play hockey.

It was 1979 and the state I was teaching in was selected to host the national education services games carnival. Since we were the host, the state's Director of Education had requested the main organizing committee to ensure that the state did well in most of the games. So, selection was held for all games and I was selected to play hockey. The team manager sent letters to all players requesting us to assemble for two weeks centralized training. We did and training started. First it was training to build our stamina followed by skills, and teamwork. Stamina and skills training went well but teamwork failed. So, one of the players suggested that we bring in a player named Bakar (not his real name) who was teaching in an interior part of the state and could not attend selection due to unavoidable circumstances. We all agreed and the player was drafted into the team and he was the sort of player our team needed.

Within days he made a 180 degree change to the team. From a disjointed side, we were finally playing as a well-coordinated team and this was because Bakar took a lot of responsibilities on his shoulders. He helped out in attack, midfield, and defence and he took care of whatever was lacking in the team to make us play like a well-greased engine.

The carnival started. We won all our matches and were in the finals. In all the matches, Bakar was the man of the match. We were all happy as we knew that second place was certain and we were satisfied to be the runner-up. If at all we won the finals, it would be a bonus. We decided to take things easy and settled to play cards. Bakar was missing. He had gone to watch the semifinal and to weigh our opponents' strengths and weaknesses. Bakar came back after the game and told that our opponents in the finals would be the team from the Ministry of Education. He added that the team was very strong and had players who were former internationals. According to Bakar, the only way we could win the game was through their left back who was slow and he pointed the finger at me.

The battle plan, as plotted by Bakar, was that he would scoop the ball to me and I was supposed to use my speed, go past the left back and send the ball into the opponents' goal area and one of our forwards was supposed to hit, flick, or push the ball into the goal box. Bakar further added that after about three scoops and hopefully three goals, they would replace their left back and bring in a player as fast as me to stop me and be my shadow. Bakar finished by saying that from then on I would be a mere passenger and the team would have to defend stoutly till the end to win the final.

It was 5 p.m. on the day of the final. The stadium announcer announced our respective jersey numbers followed by our names. When my jersey number and name were announced, I felt very happy and proud and I must thank Bakar for this. The referee blew the whistle and the final was underway. At the first opportunity, Bakar scooped the ball to me and I ran past their left back with breakneck speed and sent an inch-perfect pass into the opponents' goal area and one of our strikers pushed the ball into the goal box. Two more goals were scored in quick succession in similar fashion by the same striker. Then as predicted by Bakar, their left back was replaced with a faster one and I was a mere passenger in the team. The first part of the match strategy worked perfectly and that was the easy part. The second part was about to start and this was the difficult part and every player had to work extra hard especially Bakar.

Our opponents, realizing the damage done, came attacking ferociously and aggressively. They were firing from all cylinders but Bakar, ably helped by the other team members of the team, thwarted all attempts made by our opponents to score. Our team worked very hard to defend our lead and it was very clear that Bakar was our opponents' main stumbling block and obstacle. He orchestrated the midfield and marshalled the defence. Seeing my team mates playing so hard, I decided to abandon my position and help out in defence. But my shadow, worried that we may have some other tricks under our sleeves, followed me everywhere.

There were fifteen minutes left for the game to end and Bakar came to me and said, 'Hey! Hey! We have won' in a musical way He was confident we would win the game but I was sceptical. The pressure put on our defence by the opponents was enormous and I was worried our defence would succumb to relentless pressure. But Bakar took care of this by having answers for all our opponents' moves and tactics. Using his excellent stick work, he kept possession of the ball for long spells.

Finally the moment our team was waiting came. The referee blew his whistle and the game was over. We were Malaysian hockey champions for education services. The runner-up and winners' trophies and medals were given out. Our coach and manager took us for dinner and after dinner we returned to our rooms.

The following day we packed, said goodbye to each other and started to walk along the road to board the team bus, which was waiting to send us to the bus station. Bakar was walking a few meters in front of me and I wondered the sort of player Bakar would have been if he was not stricken with polio a few years ago and his right leg was able to function 100% instead of 30%. I thought there would not be enough superlatives in the English vocabulary to describe his skills.

This is a classic case of 'Do not judge a book by its cover' or as my Form Six teacher used to say, 'Do not pity anybody as you are not treating him as an individual.' Those who are physically impaired should be viewed as members of society and be allowed to do what they want. Help of any type and nature should only be provided when they ask for it.

He Remembers

Going to university and completing a degree was something I never dreamt of. I was a college trained teacher and teaching in a government primary school. In those days, all teachers trained in Malaysian teacher training colleges were awarded a teaching certificate and were either placed in primary or secondary schools but placed in the same salary scale. Graduates who had taken papers related to education while in university or had attended courses related to education successfully after completing their degrees were all placed in secondary schools but on a higher salary scale. I was happy with my job as it gave me a lot of free time to get involved in sporting activities. Sports, for me, was not a social activity but a competitive one where I played to win medals, trophies and other rewards. I was taking part, on a competitive level, in practically all sports played in Malaysia. I was also satisfied with my income.

However, the fire to participate competitively in sports doused due to age and at this time, sports became a social activity for fitness and health purposes. I do not know whether it was due to this change or because I was teaching the same subject at the same level for a long time but I began to feel stagnated, like as though I was running on the spot. This was when I decided to further my studies. I went through all newspapers trying to find avenues, sources, and ways to get admitted into a university, either local or foreign. My wife, who was helping me, spotted an advertisement in one of the local dailies, inviting interested candidates to pursue a degree in education through the distance learning programme. It was offered by a local public university in collaboration with a local educational institution and the requirements looked like as though the programme was tailor-made for me. It was early 1996 and I was 42 years old and married with two school-going children. I probably was at the wrong age to undertake tertiary education due to the rigours and demands of the level of study combined with family constraints. But my wife encouraged me to go for it. The next day I started the application procedure and by July 1996, I was ready for registration into the programme. On registration day, after completing all the registration processes as required by the university, all students were asked to assemble in the university's main hall. When we were all in the hall, the vice-chancellor went on stage and started his speech by saying, 'Good morning undergraduates.' When I heard the word 'undergraduates,' my head spun. I felt dizzy but it was a joyful one as I had never expected to be on the road to becoming a graduate. I told about my developments to a pastor friend of mine and he said that God has not forgotten me and in response, I could only manage a smile.

Distance learning needs commitment, discipline, sacrifice, and perseverance and I rose to the occasion quite well. Four years went by without me realizing it but before

I completed my last semester, my friend told me that I could apply for a masters programme with the results achieved thus far. This offer was from another local university and I applied. I was given a conditional offer and the condition was I must obtain a Cumulative Grade Point Average of 2.75 and above in my first degree. I completed my first degree with a Cumulative Grade Point Average of 2.89 and immediately started with my masters programme. I was 46 years old.

The masters program I had enrolled in was a mixed mode programme. I was required to complete five courses and a dissertation and to be able to graduate, I must pass all the courses with a Cumulative Grade Point Average of not less than 2.50 and pass the dissertation. For all the five courses, I had to go to the library for secondary research and present the findings and for four of the papers, there were assignments, tests, and examinations.

I finished the five courses successfully and started on the dissertation. Since I was a part-time student, I was given one year to complete my dissertation. To start a dissertation, a student must first find a topic, the problem related to the topic that needs research, and prepare a proposal. After having done this, the student, with the help of the School of Graduate Studies, must find a lecturer whose area of expertise is related to the student's area of research and is willing to supervise and guide the student until he completes his dissertation. I did everything that was required of me to prepare a proposal. It took me about three months to complete my proposal and when I took it to the supervisor assigned for me, he said that there were a lot of errors in my proposal and further added that the problem stated in my proposal did not indicate a compelling need for research and asked me to do it all over again. I felt tired. I came back home and told my wife that I felt like giving up. My wife asked me not to give up but to postpone, which was possible. If I wanted to postpone, I must write to the university expressing my intention but I did not do so. Then, like adding salt to wound, I was informed by the university that my Cumulative Grade Point Average was only 2.47 and I must repeat one course to improve on my Cumulative Grade Point Average. This meant that even though I pass my dissertation, I needed to study some more in order to graduate. The course that I was supposed to repeat was Phonetics and Phonology and I was sure I would perform poorly than the first attempt as I found this course to be very difficult. Now I felt even more tired. I just shelved my studies without any plans for it.

The university did send me a few letters wanting to know about matters regarding registration for the following semester but I totally ignored those letters. In a case like mine, after sometime, the university would automatically terminate the student's candidature and inform him via mail. But in my case, after sometime, though the period of my candidature had expired, I received a letter from the university, not informing me about termination of my candidature but asking me to see one of the main administrative officers in the School of Graduate Studies. I went and met her and very gently she told me that I had completed half the programme and there was only another half left. She requested me to complete the second half. Though she spoke gently, her words had a punching effect on me. I agreed to her suggestion and went to the administrative office to apply for extension of candidature and register for the dissertation. After completing, I left for the university's library and while I was walking, I started to think of the herculean tasks of finding a topic and related problem that indicated a dire need for research. I entered the library and went straight to the section for journals and there it was, one journal standing out of the other neatly arranged journals with a problem that I could read from where I was standing as the words were in higher case, bolded, and with bigger font size.

I took the journal and photocopied the relevant pages. Then, while driving back home, I started to think of the other aspects of the proposal and like a jigsaw puzzle, everything fell into place. When I reached home, I started to work on the proposal and within a week it was ready. My supervisor, who was different from the first person, liked it and after presenting and getting approval from the committee responsible, I started work on the dissertation proper. I went to various university libraries to gather materials and whichever library I went to, I was able to get materials easily. I used the Internet to get more materials. Usually, from my experience, I would only be successful at obtaining want I had wanted after a few attempts. But this time, I was getting them at first attempt. Help and assistance were also forthcoming with ease to do the other aspects of the dissertation and after one year, my dissertation was complete. It was read by the relevant academicians and I was informed through letter by the university that I had passed and I was happy.

But that moment of happiness was brief and it ebbed away as I realized that I had to repeat Phonetics and Phonology. I went to the registration department and wanted to register for the course but the person in charge there told me to go and see the examinations chief. I went and saw her and she told me that a meeting was held and it was decided in the meeting that to improve Cumulative Grade Point Average only, a student can repeat any course that he felt would help to improve his Cumulative Grade Point Average. It was a big relief and a burden off my head. I registered for the Graduate Seminar course and raised my Cumulative Grade Point Average to 2.53. The university sent me a letter informing me that I could graduate. I was 51 years old.

The convocation was over and one night, after a few weeks, I was sitting outside my house when I started to think. I never dreamt of university education but today I have a bachelor and masters degrees. I went down memory lane to July 1996, when it all began and started to think of all the things that took place until the time I was advised to complete my masters. The events that took place after that made me question instead of think. Why was my candidature not terminated? Why did I receive the letter to see the main administrative officer? Why was the journal standing out of all the other journals? Why was it easy for me to obtain information and help? Why was the meeting held and a new decision made? The only answer I could think of for all these questions was there were divine intervention, help, and guidance and my pastor friend was probably right that God has not forgotten me

To Believe Or Not To Believe

Don Murray or popularly known as Murray, never believed in the existence of ghosts and evil spirits. He was a happy-go-lucky kind of person who took life easy and loved to party late into the night and at parties, he was the live-wire as he was humorous and good company. He also had this ability to solve problems quickly during parties so that they would not end prematurely.

He was employed by the National Electricity Board and served in one of the board's northern region offices. On one occasion, he was sent by his immediate employer to attend a course held at the board's headquarters. Once he reached the headquarters, he and the other participants of the course were briefed about matters pertaining to the course and taken to their living quarters, which was the hostel at the headquarters. Knowing Murray, he quickly made friends and every day after the day's events, he and his new found friends would be partying. They would return about 11 p.m. and before they go to bed, all of them would wash their clothes, which was done around 5 p.m. by the other participants.

One day, after returning to the hostel, all of them were washing clothes as usual and after washing all of them returned to their rooms except for Murray. He came to wash a little late and when his friends were done with their washing, Murray continued as he had not finished yet. He was alone and while washing, he felt the presence of somebody and when he turned, he saw a man holding a human head and walking. He threw the shirt he was holding and without looking back, ran to his room. The following day he went to wash his clothes only in the afternoon and he brought a friend along. He managed to wash his clothes without giving his friend the opportunity to ask why he was washing at that hour instead of his usual washing time and why Murray had brought him along. He managed to do this by distracting him from asking these questions.

However, even after experiencing this frightening incident, Murray was still not convinced that ghosts and evil spirits existed. He thought it might have been a figment of his imagination or his eyes playing tricks with him.

Life went on as usual for Murray and with increasing age, he had slowed down on his social life. His mother advised him to get married. Initially he did not want to but finally listened to his mother's advice and got married. After marriage, Murray and his wife, Veronica, were staying with his mother. Murray's father had passed away a few years ago and as a bachelor, had stayed with his mother. Now, after marriage, he planned to stay separately but his mother did not want to stay alone in her big semi-detached house and she had requested Murray and his wife to stay with her. After a year of marriage, the newly wedded couple had their first baby, a son.

Murray's mother had good neighbors. The man of the house was David who was married to Louisa, a girl of Portuguese origin. David was involved in the cleaning business and his brothers and a few workers were helping him. For convenience sake, his brothers and workers were staying with David and Louisa.

One night, Murray and his family were sleeping soundly. Murray's mother had gone to visit her sister for a few days in another town. It was almost midnight and Murray woke up with a jolt because someone was banging on his front door. Lucky for him, his wife and son were not disturbed by the loud sound caused by the banging. He quickly switched on the front light to let the person banging the door know that he was awake and to stop banging. It worked and the banging stopped. Worried that the banging might start again and his wife and son may wake up and concerned about was going on outside his mother's house, he first opened one of the window panes as a safety measure. After seeing, he quickly opened the front door because some of those staying in David's house were standing on his mother's house porch while the others were doing something on the road in front of the house. Murray opened the grille and went to the porch to find out. With the commotion, Veronica had also woken up and joined him at the porch.

Upon seeing Murray, David came running and told Murray what had taken place. According to David, they were all watching television and Mani, one of the workers, got up suddenly, opened the front door, and started walking out of the house. They asked him where was going and he did not give them an answer. He just looked straight and walked along the road. His brothers and workers tried to stop him by pulling him back but they were unsuccessful. David added that Mani seemed to have gained enormous strength. Not believing the part about enormous strength, Murray ran to help and stop Mani and David followed closely behind. By now Louisa had come over to Murray's mother's house and stood beside Veronica.

When Murray was near, he held on to Mani's waist and pulled together with the others. Their attempt was futile and Mani seemed to drag all of them and gain distance. Then, using every ounce of their strength and energy, they pulled and Mani stopped walking. Realizing it was working, they all decided to pull continuously without stopping and they managed to bring Mani to the porch of Murray's Mother's house. They were still holding on to him as they could feel that he was still trying to walk in the same direction. Then, without any rhyme or reason, Veronica collapsed onto the fence separating both the houses and the fence bent easily since it was not secured tightly into the iron rod and when Veronica collapsed, Mani was his usual self.

Seeing Veronica down, Murray quickly ran to carry her. Veronica weighed about 55 kilograms and Murray could easily lift her using only his hands as he had lifted more in the gymnasium but when he tried to carry her, he was not even able to lift her one inch above the ground. She seemed very heavy and Murray needed the help of David and his brothers to carry Veronica and put her on the sofa in the hall of his mother's house. Veronica lay with eyes closed and motionless. No one in the hall had a hint as to what was going on. If Murray's mother was at home, she probably might know something. Murray decided to call his doctor friend to come over because to take Veronica to the hospital would be impossible as she was so heavy.

Murray started to walk to where the telephone was when Louisa started to make unusual noises. Everybody looked at Louisa. She started to stretch her hands and her eyes were widely opened and to everybody's surprise, she started to speak in Siamese. Everybody was surprised because Louisa did not know Siamese. She looked very angry.

She turned and walked at a fast pace to the kitchen and took a big mug and half-filled it with water. Then she took some yellow powder from the kitchen cabinet and mixed it with the water. Holding the mug in one hand, she walked back at the same pace and sprinkled some of the yellow colored water in the mug on Veronica's face. Immediately Veronica opened her eyes and her facial expression showed that she was wondering what was going on. Murray went towards her but Louisa stopped him and said something in Siamese. Murray did not understand Siamese and since he was still in a daze, was not able to interpret her hand actions. But one of David's brothers understood and told Murray that she wanted to know where his son was. Murray took her to the room his son was sleeping and immediately she sprinkled the yellow colored water on his face. Much to Murray's relief, his son did not wake up. After this Louisa was her usual self.

Now everything was back to normal. They all sat down and started to discuss about the day's events and tried to find answers. Nothing surfaced and David suggested that since it was late, it would be better for everyone to go to bed and seek for answers from somebody who was an authority on matters related to what they had just experienced. Everybody agreed and all of them went to their respective houses to sleep.

The following morning Murray woke up and telephoned his mother. He told her everything and asked her if she knew of anybody who could shed light on what had taken place last night. She gave him the name of a lady and also her telephone number. Murray called her. Her husband answered. Murray told him the matter and he passed the line to his wife, Agnes. After listening to Murray, she said that she would like to come to Murray's mother's house and talk to Mani. Murray went and fetched her and once back home, he called David and over the fence, told him about the latest developments. David brought Mani to Murray's mother's house. The others staying in David's house followed and she asked him what happened last night. Mani told her that they were all watching television when he heard a knock on the front door and he went and opened the door. This was all Mani could remember. He added that he did not know that he had walked out that night and only knew about it when he was told by his friends. When questioned, the others staying in David's house, who were all also watching television, said that they did not hear the knock. Then Agnes asked Mani to tell her the places he had been to yesterday. He mentioned many places and one particular place mentioned raised Agnes' eyebrows. The place uttered by Mani was Uda Gardens, a neighboring housing estate. Agnes said that she wanted to go the place and David, Agnes, and Mani got into Murray's car and with Murray driving, went to the place.

Once there, Agnes asked Mani to show and tell what all he had done there. Mani pointed to his friend's house, and told that he only went there and spent some time with his friend. The house was locked as the friend and his wife were at work. Both of them were teachers. Agnes asked about the time and Mani said that he came at about 5 p.m. and left at about 7 p.m. After listening to Mani and giving the place a look, they decided to leave. Just as they were about to get into the car, Agnes saw a tree with an antique chair tied to it. She asked Mani to come out, which he did and so did everyone. She asked if he had gone near the tree and Mani said that he did. She asked him what he did when he went near the tree. Mani said that he held the chair, sat on it, and asked his fiend to give or sell it to him. His friend refused. Agnes asked everybody to get into the car and said that she would explain everything once they were at Murray's mother's house.

They reached Murray's mother's house and everybody from David's house, eager to know what had happened the earlier night and at Uda Gardens, came over. They all sat in the hall and Agnes started. She said that Uda Gardens, before being developed, was an empty piece of land filled with lots of trees and grass. There were some houses built using wood and some of the people staying in the houses reared evil spirits known as gin (genie). They used them to do all kinds of wrong and evil activities and in return the gins were fed. If at all the master intended to leave the place, he either took the gin with him or found it a new master. If the master could not find a new master, he tied it to a tree and the other end of the string was tied to a chair for the gin to rest. If anyone disturbed it or the chair, the gin would follow the person and this person became its new master, whether he liked it or not.

So, when Mani disturbed, it had followed him and had waited for the right moment to become Mani's slave. The knock on the door was the gin knocking and when Mani opened the front door, it immediately possessed him and was taking him to a place known only to the gin. When Mani was brought back, it possessed Veronica because she was not strong. The yellow colored water sprinkled by Louisa on Veronica's face was actually holy water, which was disliked by the gin and the reason for sprinkling the same water on Murray's son's face was to protect him as he would have been possessed if the gin could not stay in Veronica's body. At this moment, a chill ran down Murray's spine and goose bumps appeared all over his body.

When Agnes finished her explanation, one of David's workers asked her where the gin would have gone. She said that it might probably have gone back to the tree. Then David asked her about Louisa and Agnes replied that since Murray's mother was very pious, the house was filled with holy spirits and one of them had descended into Louisa's body. Then David asked about the Siamese language spoken by Louisa and Agnes could not offer any explanation. She could only say that certain matters in the evil and holy worlds cannot be explained by humans.

After this incident, Murray was certain of the existence of ghosts and evil spirits. He also practiced certain rituals to ward off evil spirits from harming or following him or anybody in his family, such as asking for forgiveness when answering nature's call at isolated places and after being out at night, washing the legs before entering the house.

This issue about the existence of ghosts and evil spirits is still debated. In fact, in life there are a lot of things that are in the debatable stage. Whether you believe in it or not is not important but if by doing the needful, everybody you love is safe and happy, then it is worthwhile to do accordingly.

Giving, How Much To Give, When To Give

Part A

My maternal great grandfather had five acres of paddy land. The land was located beside the main road and in those days, the traffic volume was far less than it is now and it did not pose a danger to stay there. So, my great grandfather built a house on that land. It was a double story bungalow type house built using wood and galvanized zinc with cemented flooring. My great grandfather stayed there with my great grandmother, grandfather, grandmother, and a few other relatives. He also built a temple for Lord Rama beside the house. The temple was quite big and there was a priest to conduct the daily prayers and since it was the only temple in that area, a lot of people used to come to the temple to pray. The temple was said to be have very powerful sacred powers. Young girls, who were not married even after passing the marriageable age, got married after praying in the temple. Couples, who did not have children long after marriage, were blessed with children after visiting the temple. One couple, who did not have children for some time after marriage, were blessed with twenty-four children after coming and praying in the temple.

My great grandfather used to plant vegetables on the land for family consumption. Once a year, in the month of September or October, all family members, living in the house as well as elsewhere, would gather in the house for a special prayer. Rice, harvested from the paddy field and vegetables, grown on the land, were used for cooking the day's meal. After prayers and offering food to Lord Rama, the entire family would sit on the floor to eat. Banana leaves, cut from the banana trees around the house, were used for eating.

With time, the family size grew. Through birth, new members were added to the family and with the passing of time, they were all ready for career and marriage. My uncles went to the towns and capital city to work and my mother and aunties were married and went to stay with their respective husbands. This migration also took place in the other households there.

My great grandfather passed away and the government acquired part of my great grandfather's land for development. The number of people coming to the temple also reduced. The traffic volume had increased and my grandfather realized that it was not safe to stay in the house. He bought a piece of land in another safer and developed part of the town and built a house there. My grandfather shifted his entire family to the new house and requested an adopted uncle of mine and his wife to stay and take care of the house, temple, and land, which they did.

After some time, my adopted uncle and his wife had to leave because my adopted uncle was transferred to work in another town. My grandfather requested the family staying in the neighboring land to take care of our property and they agreed. By now, the number of people coming to the temple had reduced drastically and the temple had shrunk due to poor maintenance. We also stopped the annual family prayer as most of the family members were staying far and had commitments related to their own families. The neighboring family could not do much because they had their own land and temple to take care of. The house, which was also not maintained well, was covered with overgrown grass and creepers. One day, one of my uncle's, after seeing the condition of the house, got some workers to bring it down.

My grandfather passed away and my grandmother decided to sell the land together with the temple. They were sold and the new owner, Lingam and his family, agreed to take care of the temple but they did not. The temple was in a dilapidated condition and looked like as though it would collapse at any time. One of my aunties would always ask me to repair the temple and when I went to work and returned home, I would see the temple deteriorating daily but I was not able to do anything since it did not belong to us.

But now, although the temple did not belong to us, we restarted the annual prayer after getting permission from the Lingams. Each time we went to pray, everyone would suggest repairing the temple. So, I decided to ask permission from Lingam to repair the temple but he refused. In fact they wanted us to shift the statue of Lord Rama to another temple. They said that they wanted to sell the land for a good price and had a buyer but the prospective buyer did not want to go ahead with the transaction because of the temple. This meant that they had planned to break the temple once the statue was shifted. I did not know what to do and left everything to Lord Rama. I told about the repairing part to one of Lingam's nephews, who was staying near the temple and he told me to go ahead. He asked me not to paint the temple brightly as the current owners would know that the temple was repaired. But I did not want to do anything without getting permission.

One night, I went to bed but I could not sleep. I was lying in bed and thinking of my students when it started to rain very heavily. My thought went to the temple and I told myself that I was lying here comfortably and shielded from the rain while Lord Rama was getting wet. I decided to throw caution to wind and get the temple repaired even without permission. I was willing to face the consequences.

The next morning I met a contractor, told him everything, and took him to the temple. His estimate was RM 2300.00 for the repair. I told him to start work and asked him to paint the temple with the same color. Work started and the job was done within three days. I requested all members of the family to contribute a little, which they did and the bill was settled.

One day, Lingam came to my aunt's house. He had seen the temple and was sure it was repaired. After getting confirmation from my aunty about the repair, he started to scold her. My aunty retorted by reminding him of the promise, which he and his family did not honor. He refused to listen and told us to shift the temple and went on to say that we could have our annual prayer for that year and it would be the last one. My aunty told me and I told her to leave it to the Lord.

A few months later, we received a phone call from the owner of the neighboring land and he said that Lingam had passed away. The news went to our family members and we could not say whether he died of natural causes or through earning the wrath of Lord Rama. We were all sad. A month after the funeral, one of Lingam's sons came to my aunt's house and told us we could continue with our annual prayers for as long as we wanted. We were all happy and Lord Rama was comfortable and would not get wet when it rained

One year went by since the temple was repaired and one day, when I was at the gymnasium, my wife and second daughter came running to me and told me that new houses were going to be built on the empty land beside our house. They said that the models of the houses were displayed in the developer's office and the double storey semi-detached house was beautiful. They wanted me to see it. All three of us went to see it and it was beautiful.

At night, after dinner, my wife asked if we could buy the house. I said that we may not be able to as we were already paying for the house we were staying in. We also had a car loan and I reminded her that we had to save for our children's education. She suggested taking another look at our pay slips and see if it was possible to adjust our budget. We did and after some adjustments to the budget and taking into consideration that deduction for government housing loan would only start after the house was ready, concluded that it was possible to buy the house.

The next day we booked the house and the other procedures followed and within two years, the house was ready. We collected the keys and started the renovation process. After this we had a house warming party and moved into the house.

A few weeks passed. I was resting at home. My wife came and joined me and we were talking about our students as both of us were teachers. After talking for some time, I told my wife that our family had spent RM 2300.00 to repair Lord Rama's house and he made it possible for us to buy a house worth RM 238,888.00. I went on to say that god gives.

Part B

Mala's grandfather and grandmother came to Malaya, as it was known then, to work in the estates. They got employed as rubber tappers as there was a shortage of rubber tappers in the country. They were a very hardworking couple. Daily they woke up at 4 a.m. Mala's grandmother would prepare breakfast and lunch while her grandfather would get the tapping tools and other equipment ready. Then after washing up and putting on their tapping clothes, they would have breakfast and leave for work by bicycle. Mala's grandmother would sit on the carrier located at the back of the bicycle, holding a bag with food and her grandfather would cycle with the tapping tools and other equipment tied to the handle of the bicycle. They had to cycle about 4 kilometers to the estate's office and report to the estate workers' headman. After reporting, all the tappers would be given their respective areas to tap and they would start tapping by 6.30 a.m. On a normal day, they would tap about 400 trees and the tapping must be completed by sunrise to avoid solidification of the latex due to the heat from the sun's rays. This meant tapping fast without rest. After tapping and while waiting for the latex to flow into the cups attached, they would rest and eat the snacks, which they had brought with them. At about 10.30 a.m. they would carry two pails to collect the latex and by using a strong pole and hanging both the pails on either side of the pole, they would carry the pails and walk to the estate factory. All the latex collected by the tappers must be at the estate factory by 11.30 a.m. At the factory, they were required to pour the latex into big containers for processing by another group of workers. The tappers returned home at about 12 p.m.

On days when the management wanted more production, the tappers were required to tap about 800 trees. On these days, Mala's grandparents, just like the other workers, would wake up at about 2 a.m. and the tapping would start at about 4 a.m. Due to the darkness, they would tie small kerosene lamps or torchlights to their forehead for light and did the tapping.

Mala's grandparents were very hard working. In the afternoons, after lunch and a short rest, they would plant vegetables on the land available in front and at the back of their quarters, which was provided by the estate. The vegetables were planted for consumption and sale. Mala's grandfather, who was very thrifty, used the balance from their salaries and income from the sale of the vegetables to purchase small plots of land. At that time, an acre of rubber land cost about RM 50.00. They were buying slowly but surely.

Mala's grandparents had seven children. They went to the Tamil school in the estate and during their free time, helped Mala's grandparents in their vegetable garden. This increased income and Mala's grandfather was able to buy bigger plots of land. When the children were adults, some worked and some did not. Those who worked had jobs near their house and thus returned home every day. In this way, the family stayed together.

Mala's father was a teacher, teaching in a school nearby. One day he received a letter, which stated that he was transferred to another school. This school was very far from his house and when he told his father about the transfer, his father asked him about the distance. Since the school was far from home, Mala's grandfather told him to resign and though it involved his future, he agreed without any hesitation as he was an obedient son. His father told him he would set up a sundry shop for him in the estate and asked him to take care of the shop. Mala's father agreed.

The shop was set up and business started. Initially business was not good but later it picked up and the profit was very good. Being an obedient son, Mala's father gave the entire income to his father. From the profit, Mala's father was paid some money as salary and the remaining money was used to buy more land. The buying of land went on regularly until it came to a time when half of the total land available on the outskirts of the estate belonged to Mala's grandfather.

Time went by and Mala's grandfather was diagnosed with cancer of the throat. So, he decided it was time to write his will. He divided the land and gave everyone their share but Mala's father got less than the others because he had a shop that laid golden eggs. After some time Mala's grandfather passed away. Though everybody was prepared for his death, heavy sadness did descend on the family. It took some time for the sadness to completely evaporate.

One day, Mala's father decided to sell some of his land. He sold it to a man who stayed nearby. After the land was sold, the money from the sale was deposited into a bank and life went on as usual in the estate. One day, Mala's neighbor came over to Mala's house and told that in the land Mala's father sold tin ore was discovered. The man who had bought the land had become a millionaire. Everyone started to scold Mala's father but Mala, who was by then in her 20s, made every one calm and to accept what had happened by saying that god gives but he also knows how much to give.

Part C

Joshua finished his Malaysian Certificate of Education Examination and he was desperately looking for a job because both his parents were dead and he had to earn money to support his younger sister and brothers. He tried a few places but was not successful and his desperation could be seen from the fact that he accepted a job that paid only RM 75.00 per month. The he met a friend who asked him to join the police force, an idea which did not occur to him earlier. He applied and was successful. With the qualification he had, he could have been given the position of inspector. But he was offered the position of constable. Desperation drove him to accept it.

He was required to undergo six months of training at the police training school in the capital city. After completing training successfully, he was posted to work in the training school itself and the year was 1976. Since permanent employment was already secured, he decided to try for promotion knowing very well that he was academically qualified to be an inspector. Though academically qualified, he had to pass some papers, namely Lower Laws, which comprised of four papers and Special Laws, which comprised of three papers. Within two years he passed all the papers and applied for the post of inspector but was unsuccessful. Not discouraged, he continued to apply and promotion came but it was for the position of corporal and this only came in 1984.

Not happy with the promotion, which was understandable, he continued to apply. Though he did not get what he had wanted, his performance did not dip. He worked tirelessly and earnestly for the force and there were occasions when he ran the extra mile for the department. The hallmark of his game was loyalty. His annual appraisal for salary adjustments by his immediate superior was in the excellent category. Altogether, he had gone for interviews for the position of inspector five times and one year, in 1986, after his fourth interview, he was told he was selected. Happy and delighted, he threw a party for his friends only to be told by the force that he was not successful due to mistakes made by the interviewing officers. Dejected, he wanted to resign and accept other job opportunities offered by his friends but he talked himself out of this and plodded on with the same and undivided loyalty.

The following year, he was selected and given the letter of appointment but when he thought that he had to wait for a total of eleven years for this promotion when he could have got it much earlier, this promotion tasted flat. He accepted it and this time there was no party. After three years of service as an inspector, he was promoted to the position of chief inspector. The speed with which this promotion came did surprise him but the feeling of dejection and flat taste did not vaporize completely.

With this new position came new and more duties and responsibilities. He shouldered everything with pace not slowed, effort not reduced, and the occasional mile for sake of the force, was still run. The next level in the promotional ladder was assistant superintendent of police and just like any other regular wage earner he applied. Applications were rejected but it neither surprised nor disturbed him as he was so used to rejection and with so many officers vying for only a few vacancies, he understood and accepted the decision by the force.

His application for promotion to the position of assistant superintendent of police was successful in 2002, a twelve year waiting period after being promoted as chief inspector. When something comes long after the gestation and incubation period, then there is nothing to gloat or crow about. This was how Joshua felt. He took it as another occurrence that took place when employed by an organization or conglomerate.

The promotion increased duties and responsibilities that were more demanding than the earlier promotions. He was also transferred to a different place of work but within the capital city. The time for application to the next level of promotion, which was Deputy Superintendent of police, came and he applied but was sure he would not be successful as he would have retired by then. But his application was successful within four years. He was overjoyed and to add to his joy, the government revised the retirement age for government servants twice, which meant that he could enjoy being a deputy superintendent of police for nine years.

One day he was going to a supermarket. His daughter was driving and he was sitting beside her and the car radio was on. He leaned his head against the seat and closed his eyes just to enjoy the song. But his thought went back to 1976 and the years that came after and the events that took place. During the long periods of waiting for promotion, and being rejected, and success coming late, he had got angry with his friends, relatives, his many superiors officers, the entire force, and even god. But of course all these were kept to himself. Now he realized that they were all unnecessary as nobody was to be blamed. He also realized one more thing and that was god gives but he knows when to give.

The Turning Points

He was a primary school teacher and he taught English and besides teaching English he was very involved in sports. He used to play as well as coach the school teams in various games. In his first year of teaching in 1976, he was posted to a rural school. Though rural, the school was big with about 1,200 pupils. After the headmaster and the school's teachers got to know him, he was made the school's football coach. One of the teachers told him that though their school was the biggest, they had never been the district champions. They always lost to a school whose students were children of the natives of the country. Since they stayed in the interior, they were unaware of many things and one of it was admission into Standard One. They came when they were ten or eleven years old when the appropriate age was seven. This meant that students in Standard Five and Six were fifteen or sixteen years old.

He was unperturbed. He coached his team and as expected reached the finals. The other finalist was the school with the native children. One team had players aged twelve and the other with players aged fifteen or sixteen. He knew it would be tough but he had prepared his team well. The game started and his players played according to what he had told them. His team won and history was created.

On another occasion he was asked to form the school's hockey team to participate in the state championship. Hockey was never played in any of the district's primary schools and when the letter came regarding the championship, his school was chosen to represent the district because it was the biggest in the district. He agreed and knew that chances of doing well were very slim. This was also the opinion of the others. With the help of a friend, the selection process started followed by regular training. They went for the championship and returned home as the state's runner-up.

Since he was also playing, he had to keep fit. So, he made sure he trained daily. Every day at 4 p.m. he would put on his training gear and start training. He would jog, play volleyball, football, and badminton and would return home at 11 p.m. When he had to train the school team, he would change the schedule slightly but not the time.

Very few would do what he did to keep fit. When it came to jogging, it was not as light as jogging about two to three kilometers every alternate day or three days per week. For him, it was going round a 400 meter track 25 times or one kilometer diameter polo ground twelve times, or going up and down a four storey apartment two hundred times. The word jogging was the wrong word for what he did. It should be running because he would start slow and after completing a few laps or kilometers, would increase his pace after which he would stride and for the final few laps or kilometers, he would be running fast.

Immediately after this he would go into the volleyball court and play a few sets. For him playing volleyball was effortless as it did not involve much running and physical activity. From the volleyball court he would go to the football field and play a full ninety minute game. The position he played was midfield and for the entire ninety minutes, he would be moving all over the field. Sometimes, to eliminate boredom, he would go to the hockey pitch instead of the football field and play a full seventy minute game. Even here, he would be fully involved in the game, running up and down the right flank.

After hockey, he would go home, change his T-shirt, pack some food for dinner, and have a drink. Then, with a racquet in hand, he would go to the school to play badminton. He would go into the court at about 7.30 p.m. and come out only at about 10.30 p.m. First he would play doubles. Each time a game was over, the other three players would leave the court but not him. He would stay and three fresh players would come in. This would go on for some time and then they would switch to singles. Here again he would remain in court and take player after player. Then at about 9.30 p.m. another player would come. This bearded player was good and all he wanted were two sets of badminton with a player where lots of long rallies were possible and the bearded player knew only he could do this. At 9.30 p.m. the battle would begin and as desired by the bearded player, there would be long rallies. The never-say-die attitude was prevalent in both players and at the end of the two sets, both players would be sweating profusely. Victory would go to either one but that was not important to both but the feeling of satisfaction was. Most of the people in the town knew him as the teacher who was always in his sports shorts. This best summarized his keep-fit program.

He was also very disciplined when it came to habits. He did smoke and drink but was very controlled. He smoked three cigarettes per day and drank only three months once. When it came to competition, he never missed any game. Every Friday he went to temple to pray.

In 1980, he got his letter of transfer and he was transferred back to his home town. His fitness program and involvement in competitive sports continued but they were slowing down. He was meeting his friends in his home town after five years and he was spending time with them. Initially, he only met them at night on weekends and when he met them, he had a couple of beers. But with time, these meetings were taking place during daytime and also on weekdays. The amount of beer consumed was also increasing and so was the number of cigarettes smoked and time for fitness and sports were reducing.

He was now drinking daily and the drinking sessions started early and ended very late at night and sometimes in the wee hours of the morning. Whenever he sat down to drink, the phrase he always used was 'the day is still young.' Word spread about his drinking habit and the number of friends increased. There were days when he would have decided to have a nap once he went back home after work but once he reached home, he would receive a call and it would be an invitation to drink. It would start in the afternoon and end at about 5 a.m. Sometimes his friends would come to see him at home and when they were told he was not at home, the next question would be in which restaurant he could be in.

When it was the festive seasons, be it Chinese New Year, Deepavali, or Christmas, or functions like weddings, receptions, or birthday parties, he was sure to drink heavily. But he forgot to go to temple to pray on Fridays

His drinking affected his performance at work. He went to work late and sometimes did not go to work. When he went to work late, everybody knew he had been drinking because of the alcohol or liquor odor. When he did not go to work, he would produce a medical certificate and when he was not able to produce one, his salary was deducted.

Sometimes he would not have enough money to settle the bill. The restaurant or coffee house owner gave him credit facilities because he was a regular customer. He would settle the bills once he received his salary but there would be bills to settle the following month. Due to his drinking habit, he never saved any money. He was advised by family members to stop but he refused.

It was sad to see a person who was so health conscious and disciplined, become a total wreck.

Then, one day in the beginning of 1985, he was going to school. It was 6 a.m. Usually he rode his motorcycle to school but on that day, since he had no money to buy petrol, he took the bus. To go to his school, he needed to take two buses. The first bus would stop at a town about five kilometers from his school. From there he either got a ride on one of his fellow teachers' motorcycle or took another bus. When he was in the bus, he realized that he had no sensation on both his legs. He thought he was paralyzed and panicked. When the bus reached its first destination, he got up slowly to find out if he could stand. He could stand. Then he started to walk slowly to find out if he could walk. He could walk. Then he thought that he might not be paralyzed but blood flow to his legs might have stopped temporarily or slowed down. So, once he came out from the bus, he started to run for blood to flow in a normal manner. It did not work. Still panic stricken, he did not know what to do. He got into another bus and reached school with both his legs feeling the same way. As the morning wore on, he realized he was finding it a little difficult to remember which class he was supposed to teach.

He immediately blamed alcohol for his condition and realized that the party was over for him and these probably were the two best decisions he made in his life. That day, after work, nobody called him and even if anybody had called, he would not have gone. That day he did not drink and he did not drink for a few days. His legs felt better and memory improved. He stopped for a few months and drank again. He felt miserable as the hangover seemed to last for days and so he stopped again. He drank again on December 1985 and the following day the miserable feeling returned.

It was around this time that he met a girl and they spent a lot of time together as they had a lot of things in common. They got married and moved into their own house. He did drink but very occasionally and each time he drank, the miserable feeling would come. After two years of marriage, they had their first baby, a girl.

It was sometime since he had drunk and he decided to drink just for old times' sake. He had one too many. The following morning he woke up and was still lying in bed. His daughter, who was seven months old, came crawling to play with him. But because the miserable feeling had returned, he was not able to play with her. At once he decided that he would completely stop drinking and this was the third best decision he made in his life. He wanted to be sober and be able to play with his daughter whenever she came crawling to play with him.

A few years later he met a friend and the friend said in a very formal manner, "Thilagaraj Kandiah Muniandy, we thought you would never stop drinking but you proved us wrong."

It has now been twenty years since I stopped smoking and drinking and during all these twenty years, I feel I had been on a fast and I sincerely do not intend to break it.

Daughter To Be,
Sister To Be

She had just come to the capital town to start on her first job. Wong (not her real name), was appointed to be a clerk in the municipality. She was supposed to report on Monday but she came two days earlier on Saturday as she did not like to rush. She also wanted to see and get to know a little about the capital as this was her first trip to the capital. There was no need for her to worry about lodging as she had an uncle staying in the capital and working in the municipality also, which meant that there was also no need for her to worry about how to get to her working place.

Monday morning she woke up early. She had slept well although it was a new place. People said that you would not be able to sleep soundly the first night in a new place but she was able to. By 7 p.m. she was all dressed up and at the dining table. Her aunty had prepared breakfast and told her to start eating. But she said that she wanted to wait for her uncle and her aunty agreed. She only had to wait for five minutes as her uncle was coming towards the dining table. They had breakfast and after fifteen minutes, were on their way to the municipality.

Her uncle helped her in the preliminary matters related to reporting for work for the first time and once this was done, he left her as Wong told him that she could handle the remaining matters. She was given some instructions by her immediate boss and another officer came and introduced her to the staff sitting in the office. After this, an office boy came and took her to her table. Since this was her first day at work, she did not have much work to do and her mind drifted to her family.

Her father had passed away many years ago and her mother, who was a housewife, and two younger sisters and two younger brothers were staying with relatives in a small town far away from the capital. Her siblings were all still schooling and being the eldest, she wanted to get a job as fast as possible to support her family. Her main aim was to bring her family to stay with her as she did not want them to be burdensome to anybody because everybody had their fair share of problems and responsibilities. This did not mean her relatives were not happy to have them but Wong, even at that young age, was matured, understanding, and responsible.

She got used to work, her colleagues, the place of work, and the capital. She could move on her own within the capital and with new found friends, was feeling very comfortable and happy. She had completed one year of working. Every month, without failure, she would send money to her mother.

Her second sister finished her secondary education and was waiting for her results. In those days, the Malaysian Certificate of Education Examination results were released in the newspapers besides the schools. The results were announced and Wong, who was at the municipality, hastily checked the newspapers. Her sister had passed. She ran and informed her uncle and called her sister and congratulated her. She asked her whether she wanted to continue her studies or go to work. She wanted to work. That night she informed her uncle about her sister's intention and her uncle got her a job in a pharmacy. Her sister joined her and stayed in the same place. Though Wong was happy, a feeling of discomfort crept into her. She was beginning to feel that they might be starting to burden their uncle and aunty.

Another year passed and her third sister also passed her Malaysian Certificate of Education Examination and she also wanted to work. She told her uncle about her second sister's success and intention and this time she told that she was planning to rent a house and bring her entire family to the capital. At first, both her uncle and aunty refused. But after some discussion, her uncle and aunty agreed as they did not want to nip in the budding stage her characteristic of being responsible and they also realized that a family must stay together for the development and inculcation of values. Her uncle suggested to her to apply for a government quarters, which she did and was successful in obtaining one.

After a few months, she brought her mother, sister, and two brothers over to the capital. The house was small. It had only one room and one toilet and for six people to stay in it was going to be uncomfortable. But Wong can be stubborn if it was for a good cause and she was adamant about them staying in the house and the matter was closed. Her third sister got a temporary job.

With time, both her sisters got government jobs and it was time to for marriage. Usually the eldest got married first but

Wong had other ideas. She wanted her younger sisters to get married first as one of her younger brothers was studying in the university and being the eldest, she felt her priority was her brother's education instead of her marriage. Of course there were objections from all sides but Wong's stubborn nature surfaced and the matter was closed.

A proposal came for her second sister and after both parties had agreed, the marriage date was fixed. Wong did everything to ensure that her second sister's wedding went on without any problems. The wedding day arrived and the wedding went on without any problems. During the wedding, Wong realized that the house they were staying in, which initially was sufficient for six people, was small with more members joining the family. So, she decided to buy a house that was bigger but not for her but for the family. Using her loan facility, she bought the spacious house, which had four bedrooms and three bathrooms.

A few years later, a proposal came for her third sister and her wedding also went on without any problems. The care and concern that she showed for her second sister's wedding were also shown for her third sister's wedding. Now, it was time for Wong to get married and she had no reasons not to as her brother had graduated and working and her youngest brother was already employed by the government. She agreed and within a year, she was married and blessed with two children.

Wong was happy as she felt that she had brought her family ashore. She had taken optional retirement from her job and ventured into direct sales. She was doing very well in this area. She was happy and satisfied with the way matters had turned out for her when disaster or rather disasters struck one after another.

One day, she was driving along the highway when she heard a bang coming from the back of her car. She drove to the side of the highway and stopped. She came out of her car to check. When she came out, she saw two men standing near her car and checking it. Behind her car was their car and it was clear that they had hit her car. The two men apologized to her for the accident and asked her to check her car as they wanted to pay for the repairs. Wong inspected and noticing that there were no major repairs, told the men that everything looked alright and there was no need for any payment. But the two men insisted that she checked thoroughly and Wong, smiling and thinking that the men were so kind, started her second round of checking. As she was checking, one of the men hit her on the head with a helmet and both of them dragged and pushed her into the floor of the back of her car. One of them sat next to her and using his legs, pressed her to the floor. The other man took to the wheels.

The car was driven along the highway and during the drive, the two men asked her questions, which revolved around money. Wong, who was not only stubborn but hardy and stood for her rights, decided not to divulge information regarding money, come what may. She had money but they were hard earned money for her family and she was not willing to surrender them to these two hoodlums. Each time the two men did not receive information, she was slashed. Realizing that they would not be able to get any money out of Wong, they drove to a secluded, undeveloped part of the capital and stopped.

The two men got out of the car and dragged Wong out of the car and over a path that was covered with a mixture of sand, and big and small stones. By now, Wong had lost a lot of blood and with this rough drag, should have fainted. But steely Wong was conscious. She could see tall and short trees, shrubs, and bushes. The dragging went on and Wong thought that they were planning to kill her and dump her somewhere there. Suddenly, Wong saw two bright lights and thought that they were either accomplices of these two men or rays of hope for her. It was the latter as the two men left her and ran.

In front of Wong, stood a very big man and she saw another man, much smaller, approaching her. Though it seemed like a ray of hope, Wong was not willing to trust anybody. She plucked whatever strength was left in her and picked herself up. Through her eyes, with vision blurred by blood, sweat, and hair, she could see the big man stretching his hand out and through her ears, which were numb because of the nature of treatment received, she could hear him say something but was not able to discern meaning.

Once she was able to pick herself up, she summoned whatever energy was left in her and started to walk away from the men. She concluded that this was aimless walking but it had direction. It led to the highway and she tried to get help by waving her hand. Nobody stopped because motorists were advised not to stop along the highway except on certain areas and where she was standing, was not one of them. However, emergency patrol vehicles were allowed as they had the sirens and beacons. One vehicle stopped and this was a police highway patrol vehicle. With siren sounding and blue beacon lights rotating and flashing, the message to slow down was clear for other vehicles on the highway.

One policeman came out and after seeing her and briefly finding out the matter, helped her into the vehicle and told his partner to drive straight to the nearest hospital. In most cases, at this juncture of an ordeal, the victim would have given up fighting and collapse as there was help. But not Wong as she wanted to be aware of everything that was happening. She was willing to push her body beyond its limits.

They reached the hospital and treatment started immediately. Her wounds were cleaned and bandaged. One cut required fifty two stitches and another needed one hundred and eighty. She was admitted for observation and further treatment. Family members were informed and police officers came to take statements. After a few days in the hospital, she was discharged. She went home, rested a few days, and was driving along the same highway, with a different car. She was going to work. She changed her car not fearing her attackers but the smell of blood refused to go away even after washing, cleaning, and vacuuming many times. Any other person would have given up the job or taken a longer time before starting but not Wong. The steel in her was still shining.

Everything was going on smoothly. One night she felt feverish and thinking that it was caused by physical fatigue, she took two paracetamol tablets and went to bed. In the middle of the night, she woke up with high fever. She told her husband and he took her to the hospital. At the hospital, her blood sample was taken and sent to the laboratory. The laboratory report indicated that she was suffering from dengue hemorrhagic fever and was admitted. This type of fever is dangerous and recovery depends a lot on the body's immune system. Wong's immune system must have been good because she raised doctors' eye-brows at the rate of her recovery. She was discharged and was about to get into her husband's car, when her breathing rate increased. She was inhaling and exhaling about forty to fifty times per minute. She was readmitted and examined and the chief doctor told her husband that she was having a heart attack. He hit his forehead and looked at the chief doctor. His facial expression said it, though no words were uttered, "How could fate be so cruel to her."

The team of doctors made arrangements for her to be sent to the general hospital. At the general hospital, her condition worsened. Her red blood cell count was almost zero and she went into a coma. She was put on life support and the doctor heading the team told her family members, who were at the hospital by then, that it was a 'touch and go' situation. He told them that the dengue virus may have infected her brains and a brain scan would be done the following day. But miraculously, the following morning she came out of her coma and was normal. Doctors were surprised but happy. After a few days in hospital, she was discharged. Back home, she rested for a few days, and was off to work.

Everything was going on smoothly again when her health was affected. This time it was severe fatigue. She went to the hospital accompanied by her husband. The doctor examined her and her blood sample was taken and sent to the laboratory. The laboratory report came and the doctor read it. He called Wong and her husband into his room and told them that Wong was suffering from Myelodysplastic Syndrome, a dangerous blood disorder. The doctor said that there was not much hospitals could do about this disorder because there were no known cure for this ailment. The doctor said that research was going on in various parts of the world to find a cure for this illness. The only treatment the hospitals could provide was regular blood transfusion to make the patients feel comfortable.

So, Wong started her treatment and this illness also was not able to floor her. With blood transfusion making her feel comfortable, she went to work and did all the household chores. Occasionally, she would suffer from headaches and fatigue but she would take the pain killers prescribed by the doctors and continue to function as effectively as possible.

The headache and fatigue attacks were frequent and unbearable. She knew her health was deteriorating but she had decided to once again push her body beyond its limits. She did but this time at the expense of her life. In the early hours of 13 March 2010, she inhaled and exhaled for the last time.

Each time Wong was dealt a severe life threatening blow, she would fight back and go back to work and she went back to work to earn money. This was because when her father died, her mother and siblings were staying with relatives, who were willing to take care of them. At first, the invitation was due to sympathy but with time, this sympathy turned to anger and this anger led to family fights and the root cause of these was money. Whenever there was a fight, Wong's mother would be at the receiving end because she was not contributing financially. But Wong understood everything. She knew that everybody had commitments and responsibilities and money was needed for these. So, instead of grumbling and complaining, Wong thought that it would be better to earn as much as possible and that was what Wong did. For her, her family can have any problem but the problem must not be due to lack of money.

It was because of financial difficulties that forced Wong to be a clerk. Academically, she was good and if there was sufficient fund, she would probably have become a doctor or lawyer. But it was the dire need to earn money for her mother and siblings that made her change her career path unselfishly. When the income from her direct sales business was very substantial, she disclosed to one of her cousin brothers that she wanted to use all her income to set up a foundation for education for her siblings' children as well as her cousins' children, in view of the escalating cost of education. But death put paid to her intention.

She fought till the end and did not lose the battle but god won the right to have her.

Relatives and friends were informed of her death and many came to pay their last respects. The coffin was carried by relatives and friends and placed gently in the hearse. The hearse's door was closed and when it was ready to move, the sound of sirens blaring was heard. The sirens were from the motorcycles of two police outriders. Usually, this type of privilege or honor is accorded to presidents and prime ministers because they were considered to be very important people. But for Wong, who was neither a president nor prime minister, this honor was apt as she was a very important person for her family because a father and mother should have a daughter like her and younger brothers and sisters should have an elder sister like her.

He Never Said 'No'

I came to know Andrew (not his real name) very well when we were transferred to teach in the same school in 1989. Andrew was trained to reach Tamil and I was trained to teach English. Actually, I knew Andrew a long time ago but I would describe our relationship at that time as one based on respect for each other. We were from the same town and school but Andrew was about three years my junior. Probably it was because of this age difference that was responsible for our relationship to be described as one based on respect. Whenever we met, we just said hello to each other, exchanged a few words, and were on our way.

However, this changed when we were working colleagues. We could sit and talk at length on various topics. Andrew was involved in various societal and church activities and being elder than him, he would ask me for opinions and ideas and whenever I needed help or advise, I would totally disregard the age difference and consult Andrew as he was capable of both. Sometimes I would go to his house and we would talk for hours.

As a teacher, Andrew was in a class of his own. He was usually given the Standard One classes to teach and he would do everything possible to lay strong foundations for his students in the area of Tamil language. He was dedicated and fully committed to his profession. He followed the timetable given to him and whenever he was forced to miss classes due to meetings and other activities, he would find time and teach the students for the number of hours missed, sometimes even more. He was punctual and would try to come to school even if he was under the weather.

Students loved to have Andrew as their teacher because besides being a teacher, he was like a loving father. The other teachers would not be surprised to see a student sitting on Andrew's lap and another holding his hand and Andrew joking with them. This was something that took place on a regular basis. Without realizing, what Andrew was doing was applying Stephen D. Krashens' Affective Filter Hypothesis. This hypothesis stated that for effective learning to take place, students should not be tensed and threatened while in classroom. This is an indicator that Andrew was born to teach.

Besides teaching the students, Andrew was also very helpful. Whenever the school organized activities like sports and parents day, most of the teachers would go to him for help. Although he had his own share of duties, he had never let the teachers down. He would get the work done to their satisfaction regardless of how long it took. I had once gone to him for help and he had stayed and helped me. We finished the job and went back home at about 1 a.m.

There was an occasion when the school's headmaster wanted a classroom to be rearranged as there was to be an event that evening. It was the last day of schooling for the year and all students and teachers were happy and waiting to go home to start the long year-end school holidays. Andrew already had his hands full. Being the teacher in charge for text books for the school, he was collecting back the books, which were given to them at the beginning of the year. The headmaster approached him and told him about the event and Andrew agreed to get the classroom rearranged. He finished his job with the text books and got the classroom done and went home late without cursing and swearing at anybody.

When my father-in-law passed away, the priest conducting the 16th day prayer, a prayer conducted by all Indians sixteen days after the demise of a loved one, wanted some cow's urine. Not knowing where to get it, I asked around and a friend told me of one of the areas where I could get it. The area was somewhere near Andrew's house and I went over to his house, told him what I wanted, and asked him for the exact location. He showed me the place. The path leading to the place was dirty, muddy, and covered with grass that was knee high and since it was late in the evening, the cow shed was dark. I decided that I would go and look at other areas that were easily accessible. I turned to tell Andrew about my intention but he was nowhere to be seen. After a few minutes, he came out from his house with a bottle in hand. I told him about my decision but without saying a word and pushing me aside, he raced towards the cow shed and after a few minutes, was back with the bottle almost full with cow's urine.

He was also very helpful at home. His father was a manual worker and his mother was a housewife. He had six siblings and he was the eldest. Since his father was the only bread winner, money was in short supply. There were days when the entire family had only one meal. Andrew knew that the only way out of poverty was through education. So, besides his own lessons, he would help his brothers and sisters whenever they came to him for help.

He was also helpful to his neighbors and others in the town. Being one of the few people who was educated in the area where he stayed, he would help them by reading and writing their letters since they were illiterate, take them to hospitals and talk in English or Malay on their behalf as they were not able to talk in both the languages, and help them in matters pertaining to employees' provident fund, pensions, buying of houses, and a host of other matters. All these he would do even though he was not free or tired.

He was very devoted to his church. He never missed Sunday prayers and whenever the priest was away, he would conduct the prayers. The church made plans to build a hall and Andrew was in the forefront of this project.

Andrew's commendable characteristic of obliging and agreeing to help anybody who came to him was beginning to tell on him. There were occasions when, while talking to him, his eyelids would slowly close indicating the level of tiredness he was in. But before going into deep slumber, he would wake up and I would pretend that I had not seen him. Not to make it obvious and to allow him to rest, I would talk for a short while and leave.

It was the month of July and the year was 2001 and preparations were afloat for the Saint Anne's feast. Andrew was busy helping in the preparation. He was staying about 30 kilometers away from the church and everyday he would go and return home after finishing the days' preparations. The day of the feast arrived and Andrew was as usual very busy.

He returned home late that night and the following day he had to get up early to conduct a course for teachers. The place of the course was about 80 kilometers from his house. He woke up early, drove to the place of work, and returned home hoping to go to bed early to catch up on his sleep. Altogether, he had not slept sufficiently for about eight days.

As planned, he went to bed early and just as he was about to go into deep sleep, the telephone rang. He answered the call and it was his friend. His friend was supposed to conduct the course for the teachers the following day but due to unavoidable circumstances, he could not go and he asked if Andrew could replace him. Andrew agreed and told his wife to wake him up early the following morning. The following morning he woke up early, drove the 80 kilometers, conducted the course, and was returning home. On his way back, after he had driven about 40 kilometers, he was feeling sleepy. Before he could make any plans, like stopping the car for a nap or drink, he went into deep sleep

When he woke up, his head was over the steering wheel and his chest was against it. He lifted his head and in front of him there were two stationery vehicles, one was a cement mixer and the other was a taxi. There was a crowd standing around both the vehicles and his. It took some time for him to realize that an accident had taken place and it was his fault as he had gone into deep sleep. He tried to open the door but the door could not be opened. He looked around and realized that the car was badly damaged but he felt lucky as he was not seriously injured.

The people standing around, realizing that he could not come out of his car, telephoned the fire station and a fire engine was there within minutes. The firemen quickly got out of their vehicle, got the necessary equipment, pulled out the dented parts of the car, and got Andrew out. Once out of the car, Andrew went over to the other vehicles to find if anyone was injured. A few of them had minor bruises and the others were free from any injury. Andrew was a little shaken up and although he did not have any serious injuries, he still wanted to go to the hospital for a doctor to examine him. A friend drove him there.

Once at the hospital, he was taken into the accident and emergency department and examined by a doctor, a few hospital assistants, and nurses. They found nothing serious but told him that they wanted to admit him for observation. After admission, they asked Andrew for his house telephone number but Andrew asked them to call the hospital in his hometown as his brother was a hospital assistant there. One of the nurses called and told him the news. Andrew's brother called and informed the other members of Andrew's family and they immediately started to get ready to visit him.

Meanwhile, at the hospital, one of the nurses ran to the doctor and told him that Andrew's pressure was dropping and his pulse was low. The doctor and nurse ran to Andrew's bed and started treatment but it was too late. Andrew passed away and he was only 45 years old. The nurse who had called earlier called his brother and told him the sad news.

Andrew's family members were about to get into their car when the telephone rang. One of his sisters answered the call and when told of the news, she was rooted to the ground and not able to say a word. When the others saw her, they came running to her to find out what had happened. Andrew's sister hugged Andrew's wife and started to cry. Still not certain as to what had taken place, Andrew's mother held her arm and asked her and this time she was able to speak and she told her that Andrew had passed away.

News of Andrew's untimely death spread and everyone who heard it was shocked and deeply saddened. When I was told about this news by my neighbor, I sat down on a chair and was wondering how he could possibly die so early. He had a lot to offer to his family, friends, church, town, and society.

I went to pay my respect one day before the funeral as I was supposed to be elsewhere on the day of the funeral. I was told by a friend that the funeral looked like a festival as the crowd was large. Police help was sought to control the crowd and traffic.

After the funeral, I met a teacher who was known to both Andrew and me. He told me that when Andrew was in the accident and emergency department, the doctor asked him whether the accident occurred because it was the fault of one of the drivers of the other two vehicles. Andrew said that it was his fault as he had slept while driving.

Even when death was knocking at his door, Andrew was in a class of his own.